SALT
A GU

All text and pictures by Simon Palmer

Dedicated to my Mother, June

First Published 1996 by Salts Estates Limited
Salts Mill Saltaire West Yorkshire BD18 3LB
01274 531163

© 1996 Jonathan Silver
ISBN 0 9516950 5 3

SIR TITUS SALT BARONET (1803-1876)
The Great Philanthropist

Titus Salt as a young man thought of becoming a doctor. This plan was thwarted when doing some carpentry he cut himself and fainted. So he went into trade with Messrs. Rouse's under the guidance of John Hammond. When he was qualified he joined his father as a woolstapler. Outside his expected duties he experimented with different fibres. On one occasion he bought a bale of Donskoi wool from Russia, tried to interest other mills in this wool (new to the English trade), however no one would buy it. Undefeated he tried himself, creating his own unique blend and then wove it into worsted fabric. The result was a fine quality cloth and with it, Titus Salt's first big success.

This personal achievement gave Titus the confidence to ask the woman he loved, Caroline Witham, for her hand, and they were married in 1830.

There came a cotton famine in Lancashire caused by the American Civil War and it seemed set to last. People began looking for alternative raw materials. Titus joined in the search for a cotton substitute, finding his answer in a redundant bale of smelly, greasy fleeces at Liverpool's Albert Docks. It turned out to be alpaca from the Peruvian llama. Titus Salt cleaned it up and experimented again, and after some trials and tribulations he produced an exciting new yarn, the result of combining alpaca with Yorkshire wool, producing a worsted, cloth with a lustrous sheen. This proved hugely popular with the ladies fashion trade of the time.

As well as having a disciplined desire to succeed, Titus Salt, a devout Congregationalist, was a gentlemen of strong religious principles and compassion. The working and living conditions in Bradford had become increasingly disgusting, caused by the exploding Industrial Revolution. He dreamed of a Utopian settlement and bought a green-field site near the river Aire, located between the Leeds Liverpool canal and the railway. By 1853 his 'state of the art' mill was ready for action, designed by Architects Lockwood and Mawson.

As Sir Titus Salt's success continued, so did his philanthropy. He built good clean houses in his model village, next to the mill, for his workforce. The Congregational Church, a school, the mechanics institute, sports facilities, recreation ground, infirmary, baths, wash houses, and almshouses followed.

And they called the place SALTAIRE.

THE HOUSE WITH TWO NAMES

This building is at the top of Victoria Road in a terrace with the main hospital building at the other end. There is a charm these buildings possess that others in Saltaire have sacrificed in favour of grandeur.

Sitting down to draw this building brought the eye level right down and because the land is rising it had the effect of making the surrounding environment appear insignificant. It gave the impression of being on a summit, of some out of the way, remote place (ignoring the noisy traffic on Bingley Road to my right). It reminded me of the stationmaster's house and waiting room of an isolated railway station on the moors.

There is the present road name on this house, (on the junction with Bingley Road) but by the upstairs windows is an older sign that escaped being removed, enamel blue and white, although I don't suppose it is the original, maybe it is. More likely from the 20's or 30's; so because of this time travel connection it appealed to me to superimpose some figures from another era, which is in fact the 1930's.

THE ALMSHOUSES
April 1996

Above the hospital the almshouses stretch the upper length of Victoria Road between the main thoroughfares Saltaire Road and Bingley Road. Behind the hospital the almshouses face on to the pavement but on the west side they are set back with their own loop road providing the folk with a quiet residential haven.

They were originally opened in 1868 for people of good moral character who were incapable of work for reasons of age, disease or infirmity. They were provided with all 'mod cons' although no central heating in those days. A little chapel was built so they didn't have to walk all the way down to the congregational church and also had no excuse not to attend services.

All residents received a weekly allowance, which perhaps not all mill owners were prepared to do for those no longer able to labour for the industry.

I liked this view of one of the corner almshouses with the lawns and conifers in front, and where there would be roses in summer borders. It was a late Spring and the daffodils were not even in flower when I knelt on the damp grass. This picture needed full areas of texture to give it body, unlike for example, the drawings of Shipley Glen Tramway.

THE HOSPITAL

It was inevitable that with Titus Salt's generous provision for his workforce he would include an infirmary among the facilities, for people exposed to the risk of various accidents from machinery. Presumably, on account of his attitude towards excessive drinking, people nursing hangovers were strictly forbidden medication.

The hospital or infirmary like the almshouses was opened in 1868 and echoes the same architecture. There is a photograph sitting in front of me on my desk of it in its original state before a third storey had to be added between 1908 and 1909. Perhaps people were growing more accident prone; a forgivable oversight on the part of the architect.

The drawings on the opposite page are not strictly of the hospital but these details relate to it as much as to the almshouses, the little motifs repeated throughout the building complex.

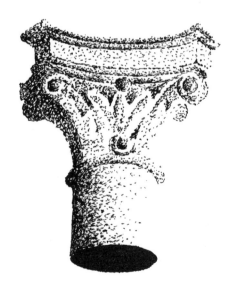

HOSPITAL
1868

OPENED
TEMBER
1868.

S.P.

SIR TITUS SALT'S TOWER
7th May 1996

If you walk down Victoria Road, before the school turn left into Titus Street where you will come to the house with the extra room. To me it has a nautical feel. I expect to see a coast guard or someone in a navy blue uniform with binoculars, looking out onto a rough sea. The reason perhaps because of its robust appearance (as if to withstand the force of an aggressive south westerly or an exceptionally high tide).

Apparently Titus Salt employed somebody to survey the town, presumably to look out for trouble makers on a Saturday night or washing drying on the line on Sunday. Whatever the problem or concern, no doubt it was reported back to Mr Salt for his attention. Equivalent to a latter day close circuit T.V.

I must recount a bizarre moment as I drew this building, on a Sunday morning in May. Someone appeared in the tower room, dressed in a uniform similar to that of the Salvation Army. The grey gentleman wore a 'handlebar' moustache and a monocle flashed reflected light. He kept looking at me and then at what was possibly a list of names or identification records. I kept working on the drawing, trying to appear as innocent as possible but when I looked up, the man had gone.

GEORGE
STREET

VICTORIA ROAD
Tuesday 16th April 1996

Victoria Road is the main artery with residential streets feeding off to the east and west of Saltaire. It is the southern access route to shops, the mill, railway station, college, the canal, river and the park. Despite the demand on Victoria Road the pace always feels relaxed.

Today I arrived early and before wandering up to the almshouses, while it was still quite quiet, I produced this drawing looking north with the mill beyond. Although cold, the sun was shining, it felt quite continental – like a boulevard, with the avenue of trees and style of buildings.

In the summer the broad leaves of the chestnut trees shade the four lions that guard the school and institute. In this drawing the head of 'war' is visible outside the institute his companion to the south corner is 'peace', opposite are 'vigilance' and 'determination'.

Apparently these lions were destined for Trafalgar Square. It was either they were too small or a conflict or misunderstanding with Sir E. Landseer led them to grace Victoria Road.

TWO LASSES AND TWO LLAMAS
Early May 1996

Both decorations opposite each other. The more sculptural adorns the front facade above the door of the Mechanics Institute, completed in 1871, but now known as Victoria Hall. It represents the sciences and the arts. Sir Titus Salt had the institute built for the inhabitants of Saltaire to broaden their horizons when not working and to discourage them from less favourable temptations. Although he was not trying to enforce total abstinence Sir Titus Salt felt public houses nurtured antisocial vices so he would not be persuaded to build any in Saltaire. So if you fancied a pint in a pub you would have to bike it to Bingley or cycle into Shipley.

Opposite the institute, a bas relief decorates the central gable of, the school built three years earlier. Sir Titus Salts concern for the welfare of his workforce included education for the children. However only the very young received full time education. They were not very old before they began part time working in the mill with lessons the rest of the day.

Both decorations sport the Salt coat of arms and although recognisably the same heraldic motif, they are subtly different.

The llamas on the bas relief look very proud quite rightly so as they played a strong part in the success of the Saltaire phenomenon

ALBERT TERRACE

Albert Terrace runs along the north perimeter of the estate and looking west to more open country, Cross Gates and Harden Moor. Below the terrace a midmorning metro departs from Saltaire. The station provides an easy and convenient approach from the Leeds Bradford conurbation and the more rural Keighley and Skipton. From Skipton there is a connection with the famous Settle – Carlisle run through the exciting and beautiful Ribbledale.

To the right of the picture is George Street with the west facing terrace backing up to the east facing terrace of William Henry Street. The backs of the houses each lead to a small yard with an alley running down the middle separating the two terraces.

Some yards have become utility squares for dustbins and rotating washing lines, others have become cultivated little gardens or patios with potted fuchsias, geraniums and lobelia. Whatever their use or purpose every other one of these yards seems inhabited by a cat.

This Victorian housing estate will have changed little since it was built (1867). Perhaps the obvious differences being P.V.C. replacement windows, multifarious styles of front door, the ubiquitous T.V. aerial and a growing number of satellite dishes. However there is a conservation scheme initiative run by the local authority and gradually the houses in the village are being returned to their former glory. Grants are available to refurbish doors and windows.

THE NEW CHIMNEY
April 1996

When the extension to the mill was built by the river Aire, objections were voiced regarding the new chimney, arguing it would detract from the view on that side of the premises. The solution was to design it like an Italian campanile and is in fact a copy of the church tower of Santa Maria Gloriosa in Venice – problem solved.

Wandering around the grounds of the congregational church, having just drawn a railway train, I noticed this different vista of the chimney and decided on a drawing before the foliage of the trees obscured the view.

THE CONGREGATIONAL CHURCH

Work began in 1858 and the church was completed just one year later, so the builders and joiners must have been working for bonuses. For that time the cost topped £16,000 which must have seemed extravagant, although now you probably couldn't buy a decent garage for that amount. It was because of Titus Salt's dedication to Congregationalism that no expense was spared in the planning and the building of the Church so that it really does..... 'stand like a palace for God'

It is the most elaborately decorated of all the buildings in Saltaire. The porch, for example supported by fine Corinthian columns and above them further columns terminate in a leaded dome housing the clock chimes.

When the church is open, don't hesitate to enter. Friendly members of the United Reformed Church will probably be there to answer any questions or offer an information board describing the building in detail.

The family mausoleum is down on the south (I have my doubts about their guardian angel) tucked under the balustrade which encloses communion table, pulpit and organ.

THE WEIR

From Gordale Scar high up in the Yorkshire Dales, the River Aire begins its journey south east; through Gargrave (where it is joined by the Leeds and Liverpool canal), Skipton, Keighley before it passes Saltaire and on through Leeds to join the River Ouse just North of Goole.

The Aire like many dales rivers flows fast by English standards. This is especially noticeable in the winter after a rapid thaw produces 'melt water' and when combined with heavy rainfall it really creates a 'spate' and thunders over the weir.

The weir at Saltaire (there is another upstream at Marley) helps to control floodwater by regulating the level upstream, hopefully reducing the risk of flooding further down river.

The building to the right of the weir is the 'new extension' built sometime after 1853. It was the new spinning mill and dyeworks erected on the old site of Dixon's Mill. The planned siting of this mill right by the River Aire was to utilise the water more effectively for power. The supply of water proved however to be too irregular for practical use. Now the mill has been occupied by Bradford Health and there are flats alongside.

In Roberts Park the bronze statue of Sir Titus Salt by J Derwent Wood stands proud on its plinth. On the plinth is an inscription and bas relief of the mill, a South American llama from which comes the lustrous alpaca wool and the angora goat, on the other side, from which comes mohair.

'OPEN AT TWELVE'
Friday 7th June 1996

Visited Shipley Glen Tramway on Tuesday 4th June but did not have the time to complete any significant drawing. So returned on the Friday and found it closed. Paul was either clearing the track of dandelions or harvesting them for a rabbit when I walked past up the hill. He said I could climb over the fence once I reached the top station. It was mid morning just after refreshing rain, quiet and a lovely subject to draw – all lines and signs.

This picture suited black line work alone, avoiding the additional use of tones of cross-hatching and heavily worked textures. Although I have created texture for the trees, as a background a more widespread use of texture and cross-hatching would have simply muddled the composition, making it harder to read.

27

THE PAVILION, ROBERTS PARK
7th May 1996

Walking back down after drawing the Shipley Glen Tramway, on my way to Hirst Lock, skirted Robert's Park down by the river and thought the Pavilion well worth drawing. The chestnut trees were late and were only just coming into flower. The composition is made more interesting with the score board just to the left, with sharp perspective and the numbers and lettering make for a good graphic piece of work.

Cricket matches are still played although it is confusing, Saltaire having two cricket grounds. Although there has never been a match played when I have visited Robert's Park, I could not resist putting a score on the board with two batsmen making use of the Pavilion.

An alternative title to the picture could be:

'Opening Batsman Suffers a Humiliation'

THE FOOTBALL GROUND
Friday June 7th 1996

After drawing the pavilion in Robert's Park I
continued along the path by the river towards
Hirst Lock. The sky was very heavy and
threatening, the forecasted rain arrived as I crossed
the bridge over the River Aire close to Hirst Lock.
I sheltered in one of the stands overlooking the
football pitch.

This picture was quite serendipitous in a sense.
While I waited for the rain to pass I started drawing
and an interesting view of the congregational
church and mill chimney began to emerge.

HIRST LOCK

It was good to return to Hirst Lock, this time on foot and sadly not by boat.

On 12th October 1995 we had hired a boat from Snaygill, just outside Skipton for a weekend cruise. One of the purposes of the trip was to approach Saltaire by a route other than road or rail. We departed Thursday evening and tied up after dark. Friday was trouble free but countless swing bridges made travelling slow. Started on Saturday 14th at seven o'clock in the morning and reached Bingley by nine. Due to the Summer drought that continued late into Autumn the locks were padlocked until ten. It took three hours to reach Saltaire, a distance under two miles but with eleven locks.

It is not until you reach Hirst lock that you can really see the mill chimney and the rooftops of Albert Terrace appearing above the trees. Once through the lock it is no more than ten minutes to Saltaire – the appearance of the congregational church is a delight, especially as I remember it last October with the Autumn colours.

S.T.

MILNER FIELD, GILSTEAD

All that remains of this ill-fated gothic pile, just
some lintels, masonry and when not swamped
by summer undergrowth, traces of mosaic floor
from the grand hallway or possibly the huge
conservatory.

The house or more aptly, the mansion developed a
malign atmosphere when three of its occupants
were afflicted with premature deaths. Firstly Titus
Salt (Junior) at the age of 45 who built it, followed
later in the 1920's by Ernest Gates and A.R. Hollins
both at the age of 47. The house was put on the
market in 1930 but nobody seemed eager to
purchase it so it was demolished in 1950 by which
time it would have reached a very poor state of
repair.

There is some reference to Milner Field in 'Brass
Castles' by George Sheeran (Ryburn). A
reproduction of the front elevation reveals what an
imposing gothic structure it was, and an inset
engraving 'View from the Park' how it must have
dominated the skyline above the park and
woodland. Two old photographs which are
reproduced in the book are dark, something about
them sinister and more than a touch spooky.

Now it has been flattened and is overgrown. Just
the gatehouses, south and north remain. The South
is occupied, the North gatehouse bricked up, dark
under the trees and itself a little eerie.

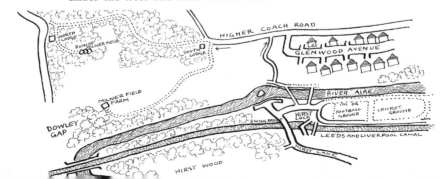

34

THE MAIN ENTRANCE TO SALTS MILL
August 1995

Usually the busiest stretch of Victoria Road, with people coming to and from work. All manner of delivery vans and expensive looking motors arriving or departing. People making their way to the park for recreation, or pupils returning from the grammar school just beyond Robert's Park on Higher Coach Road. Despite this activity it rarely feels frenetic. There is generally a relaxed atmosphere helped by the fact Victoria Road is no longer a thoroughfare and perhaps the cobbles help to slow traffic down or they have seen the ice cream van parked on the bridge.

If you visit Saltaire by train, the main entrance to Salts Mill is just to your left as you come up from the station, and the west face of the great mill is directly in front.

If you arrive by Leeds and Liverpool canal, tie up by the bridge, the main entrance is just to your left. Find your way round to the side and explore the mill where you may catch strains of music coming from behind the great door of the 1853 gallery. Ahead, a stairway leads to a variety of shops on spacious floors. The Diner on the second floor provides a selection of refreshments and meals. All of the public spaces are open every day except Christmas and Boxing Day from 10 until 6.

THE 1853 GALLERY

The 1853 Gallery is overflowing with David Hockney's pictures. It is a delight to see some of his very early work, oil paintings and drawings and the etchings of the Rake's Progress (the first work of his I think I ever saw). Photo-collages and stage designs, an eclectic mix of work but all very Hockney. My favourites (this week) are the lithographic portraits. The output of work is overwhelming; his work spanning time from when a young boy to the present day. I can imagine his art master in the common room some years after David had left Bradford Grammar School saying 'I told you the lad had talent'.

You may lose all track of time wandering around this gallery, engrossed in the pictures, lost amongst the acres of books which are laid out on a variety of interesting pieces of furniture, (far preferable to rows of cramped bookshelves). The mill has the advantage of space. Space that envelops you, listening to the sound of Wagner or other fine music. Arias and orchestras come to meet you from behind pictures and plants, chairs and chests.

There are two more galleries upstairs showing recent work. However, before you embark on this exhibition expedition, you will have to finally extricate yourself from this wealth of pictures, literature and music. After the postcards, Burmantofts pottery and the heady scent of the lilies you will need to boost your batteries upstairs in the Diner.

THE DINER

It is perhaps now a good opportunity to thank Mr Jonathan Silver for granting me permission to use the Salts Diner on the 2nd Floor of the mill. It should be pointed out that he has taken a huge risk and has agreed to take full responsibility for my sudden outbursts of embarrassing behaviour. Its rather convenient that the diner is open 7 days a week nine to six.

The staff of the diner have coped with me admirably and have remained amazingly calm in reassuring other customers, persuading them not to run away when I am at my most pitiful. On my arrival, usually unannounced and without prior warning, Nigel will discreetly escort me to a corner where my presence will do the least harm, behind a tree with which I have had many conversations and have enjoyed its company, sharing a cigarette.

Did you know the rumour is true that when the chefs are not too busy they take their trousers off, lay them on the floor and use them to play a unique two pronged game of chess.

There is another interesting point regarding the Diner, which is they used to serve crocodile steaks until a truly strange phenomenon occurred. Celia, who now stands in suspended animation on the long counter did a very brave act. It was one Wednesday lunch time, at about 12.45 (I know because I was there watching from behind my tree) Celia plucked up the courage to walk across to a table where they had just ordered four crocodile steaks and said the following thing in perfect French. 'Est-çe-que vous savez que çela est ma mère que vous allez manger?'

Llama casserole is also off the menu – but that is another story.